I dedicate this book to my family and friends. You all have

inspired me to follow my dreams.

I love you all and thank you for loving me.

-Monda

S0-FCA-809

From the Author

I am not writing this book for recognition or fame. I am writing this for you-- the girl inside the woman who struggles with her insecurities and the boy inside the man that is scared to live out his dreams. I am sharing a part of me to inspire you to follow your heart.

Every line of this book reflects my life in its entirety up to this point. Come with me on a transformational journey led by God. You will witness His works through me on every page.

This life hasn't been easy, to be honest it gets tougher day by day, but the amount of peace and joy that I am finding surpasses the struggles I face.

Read each line as if they mean more than the phrases they form. Read them as if they were a hug you needed to assure you that you're not alone. Read them as if they were the ointment you need to heal an open wound. For these lines are More Than Words. This is my life, my thoughts, and my journey.

Enjoy.
-LaMonda A. Sykes

Table of Contents

My Life...

Her

I caught myself comparing myself to a woman I didn't know;

I've never spoken a phrase to her.

I sat and imagined that her life was full of sunny days.

Unlike the rain clouds that periodically filled my mornings.

She was so beautiful;

Her eyes were overflowing with promise and ambition.

She laughed, a beautiful melodic sound, as if fear was the butt

of a joke she just recalled.

I wanted to get closer to her,

I had to figure out her methods of living.

I just needed to be in her presence.

An envious moment turned to a scary obsession.

The more I stared at her the more I realized she was me and I,

she.

We were one in the same.

I, my insecurities, and she, everything I imagined being....

Nostalgia

The crispness of fall reminds me of the move.
Only four years old when my mother explained the transition
from life to death.
Streams of lights cut through clouds, beaming on the souls of
the resting
As our Buick swerved through the winding roads of the
Appalachian trails.
I tried to understand the beginning of my new life.
In my short time of living, I went from being the only child
living in the Midwest,
To becoming a sibling to cousins I never met.
Shy, I was. Quiet as ever.
"They talk funny", is all I can remember telling my
grandmother in Illinois.
Long distance calls were rituals in my weekly routine.

Fire color leaves surrounded our quaint home as smoke filled
the air from our chimney.
Stories of life lessons told by my ailing grandfather,
Thanksgiving dinners, Christmas bike rides up a dirt road,
Playing on gravel hills afterschool,

3

Honeysuckles every spring, chasing fire flies during the warm
summer nights.
Turning over new soil, playing with earth worms,
Foot races and basketball games filled my weekends.

Then it all changed, changed again.
I witnessed death up close and personal.
My stepfather, lying sleep in their bed, shifted from our home
to his next.
Starring at him subconsciously, but physically my body moving
trying to stay calm and calling 911.
Family members running in our home to rescue us from crying
alone.
I couldn't sleep.
Night after night, I saw his face sleeping…he wasn't breathing.
How can a man who lived with us for four years be gone?
My mother's husband had left, leaving us with the goodbyes
from the morning.

Falling leaves, smoke filled airs, holidays, and crisp nights all
remind me of how my life changed forever.

Wishin'...

I wish you were here;
To tell me I was your precious baby.
To squeeze me tight when the weight of the world seemed too
hard for me to bear.
I wish our conversations lasted longer than a simple hi and bye,
I wish I had you to simply say goodnight.
No other has filled the space in my life;
I've tried to add him, subtract them;
But none could ever occupy the void you've left.
Who knew grieving could last so many years.
Shallow thoughts of self, not knowing my true worth.
It's not fair;
Others have theirs…and mine's, a phone call away
Will never be there.

The First Time...

I thought the only way to keep you was to give you a part of

me no one has ever had.

I thought sacrificing my sacredness would show you how much

I cared for you.

I thought allowing you to penetrate my secret place gave me

all of you.

Instead it gave you all of me.

When you left you took my innocence.

You opened my eyes to a world I didn't know.

Without warning you abandoned me in a place that I had to

seek validation

By opening up again and again...

Again, to a man who didn't value my gift.

You left me vulnerable and alone, scarred.

I thought giving you a part of me would make you stay.

Release

Last night, I let go.

Let go of the notion of you and I.

I've always said I wanted to be in love and then I realized I

was.

I was in love, you didn't reciprocate.

I tried to understand your reasoning, but your priorities didn't

include me.

That's fine.

You stayed true to yours now I'm living my truth.

I loved you wholeheartedly, no regrets.

I wish you all the best, but I let go.

395

Back and forth I've tossed with this notion of our "situation-ship".

Months ago I declared I will be pursued by the man that will truly want me.

I am no longer settling for the boy I have to chase.

Then that night…

My flesh was screaming it needed your attention.

I dialed your number and we planned the main event.

395 days since we've partaken in this dance.

395 days I've longed for you.

395 days no one else has entered the ring with me

I was about to throw it all away in one day…

DAMN!

I did it again. I took matters into my own hands.

In two days, for one night,

I was going to end my sacrifice for a boy that hadn't shown me what I deserved.

Hadn't shown me that I was worth the chase.

Hadn't shown me that I was worth a phone call over the last 395 days!

But my flesh?

What about my heart?

My passion would be satisfied for the moment but what about

the confusion that will last a lifetime?

It took me 395 days to regain my strength.

395 days to rebuild my confidence...

Do I really wanna throw it away for one night?

Full Moon

7 a.m. still sitting high.

Waiting to be noticed.

The night she rose, she came with a massive wind

Making her presence known.

But for how long?

Wanting, needing, YOU, him, her

She awaits your attention.

Days pass and you haven't noticed her fullness,

She begins to dwindle.

7 turned to 1 and she disappears.

Lost in the darkness of the bright lights this world shines.

She's lost in the chaotic space you call life.

Finally you noticed, too late.

Her glowing demeanor and loving nature no longer reigns

supreme.

Until randomly, she builds herself up again.

Full body standing complete once again...

Waiting for you to notice her...

Undecided

I wanted to love you,

Not knowing exactly what that entailed,

But you intrigued me.

My curiosity sparked by your smile, your walk, and intellect.

Our conversation, brief, sparked a part of me never touched.

I wanted to love you.

Not knowing exactly what that meant,

You stood confidently in a mass of normalcy.

Strong presence, calm demeanor,

You stood out and fitted in perfectly.

I wanted to love you.

Not knowing exactly what that could do.

I feared changing myself to include all of you.

Your life could possibly shift my world without any effort.

I couldn't let you. I had more living to do.

I chose not to love you.

My Thoughts…

12

#hashtag

I look at these pictures wondering if this is the life that I should
aspire to live.
Should I be the dope bad ass bitch that some are perpetrating
to be?
Or should I live freely with no cares of the world as some post
so frequently…
No, no, nooooo
I need to #riseandgrind and #nevasleep
So I can #getthismoney
#givingmelife
No #givemetruth
Our images portray a life we all wish to have—unflawed and
filled with our heart's desires.
But, I don't know what to believe.
I #wakeup to see that I am still asleep because society is
constantly poisoning me
Who are we to #challenge each other to be vain…
Or be disrespectful?
Why have we determined our value based off a like?
#repost 'cause it sounds good, but are we living by the quotes
that paint our TL's?

#nocomment

Let me take a selfie…#nofilter.

I Cried

I cried today.

I mourned like a mother who lost her son,

Like a father who can't save his daughter.

I cried.

On my hands and knees asking why am I seeing this,

Why are we fighting this?

Who are we fighting against?

Is this real or are we in a different dimension?

I cried today because this isn't a physical war anymore.

It never was.

The spirits of good and evil are at odds like never before.

I cried today because I feel I am the only one who sees it.

I mourned because I'm stuck in between.

Father God I need you, Christ come save me....

With tears falling down my cheek,

I cried.

Track List...

What have I been listening to?
Nothing much really…
The **History** album is constantly playing in rotation,
The group **"Lies and Unheard Cries"** has filling my ear
phones.
"Will I die or will I live", is the name of their latest track.
Yo', listen to these lyrics:

*"I'm no different from these men; my actions are
considered a sin, when daily they murder harmless
babies...sons and daughters, weeping fathers and
mothers. Breathing is a blessing, but we are in a war
zone, I can't call this place my home when they are
aiming to kill me, equal opportunity with limited
liability... my complexion separate us but we're supposed
to stand united...right?"*

WHAT!? That verse gets me every time!
"Only the Lord Knows" and *"Unarmed but My Skin is a
Target"* are my favorite songs.
On a daily I play *"God, could I be next?"*

It's my anthem—man I can't leave the house without hearing
it.

Then I have a little gospel, you know to ease my soul.

"You Can Breathe Again" and ***"Lifted Hands"*** are the two
songs that give me peace when my days are stressful.

It puts me in a safe space when the world becomes cold...

I'm thinking about coppin' this new joint called

"I Pray"...sounds like it's a must have!

But yeah...my track list is simple.

When?

When will I get tired of tasting my own blood?
Biting my tongue to spare your feelings has become so
mundane.
You don't mind speaking your peace;
When will I get tired of seeking your permission?
I was giving as much dominion over this world as you
In fact, more! Since I've happened to birth nations.
When will I get tired of letting my physical appearance define
my worth?
Makeup can't hide everything, weaves itch and my waist ain't
supposed to touch my ribs.
When will I stop allowing my sons, fathers, and brothers, to
call me out my name?
Last time I checked, dogs and I weren't comparable.
When will I see my sisters, mothers, and daughters as beautiful
equals instead of ugly competition?
We all desire to be loved and to love our beautiful creations.
When will I accept my flaws as unique definitions of me
instead of targets to be laughed at?
We are all created in His image.
When will I stop asking when?

When the time is right?

Maybe

Maybe my way of thinking is harmful to your way of living,

Maybe my love for you affects your results,

Your words say you want change but your actions repeatedly

say different

Our friendship feels like a Ferris wheel...

Going around and around—not diving into the real issues.

Maybe I am to blame.

Maybe I was too sensitive to your feelings that I never told you

the truth.

Maybe it's my fault for expressing my frustrations behind your

back instead of to your face.

But how can I be honest when you push back so heavily?

Maybe we aren't as close as we both thought

Maybe we are too close

Maybe I pick at your imperfections because they mirror the

flaws I try to hide.

Maybe I hold you to a certain standard because of the

expectations I have for myself.

Maybe I should distance myself so you can live your life.

Maybe I should be closer so that you know that I am by your

side.

Maybe I should just let things be
I pray for you daily, hoping one day…
One day, maybe.

Praying...

Dear God,

I'm trying to play catch up.

Racing to get back where I should've been, but I keep tripping

Falling over lies, stomping my toes on false hopes,

This isn't me.

But why do I keep trying to go back there?

They've said I am wise beyond my years.

But this wisdom tends to leave me alone.

In solitude, I questioned my existence,

I questioned why You would let me be here hidden.

Stuck in limbo...

Not able to relate to the struggle and not able to say I am fully

successful.

I'm just here. With my paper and pen,

Wondering where I fit in?

The past no longer, the future unknown.

My present, a present being wasted with anxiety and

questions.

Grant me serenity, grant me understanding.

Help me to trust Your perfect plan.

Live (Audience's Perspective)

Big stage.

Fans causing a rage to see you fall.

Your last performance left them speechless; they just knew an encore was inevitable.

But you said you didn't do it for the onlookers, spectators.

You said you did it for the love, the euphoric feeling.

You said it was like being next to God every time you performed.

But what you failed to tell your fans was you were dying inside...

The only way to relieve your ache and loneliness is to perform On this stage.

The stage you called life.

The agony of exiting causes you terrifying visions...

So you extend your show by being cautious, and keeping it all in line.

Is this alleviating the pain you're feeling?

Nah, can't be.

It seems like denial is finally catching up with you.

Pleasing your audience's desires to defame your name is slowly suffocating you.

Causing you to become complacent.

Walk away my brotha...please drop the mic my sista

It is okay if they don't recognize your efforts.

It is okay if they will never know your name.

All that matters is that your gift—that has been divinely placed

in you is used in truth.

LIVE BABY LIVE

For a world that's dying.

Live for a world that will never know true love and peace.

Live...baby...live.

My Journey...

Current State... (Voice of the performer)

The dynamics of this world are changing
Or maybe it's my world making a shift.
Drive and passion lie dormant in the attic of my mind.
Deferred dreams are substituted by the suffering that society
brings.
I've become complacent, I stand still hoping my dreams would
manifest without any effort.
Standing paralyzed with fear because the opinions of others
weigh more than my own

Where is my confidence? Where is my belief in self?
I need a push to take the first step.
All I can sense is time running away...
The world changing and I am staying the same.

Hindsight

Growing up isn't easy.

Losing sight of who you truly are to form and fit perfectly in a box created in the minds of weak individuals.

Your self perception is worth the value of the last dollar you made.

So driven by cents, that you've lost all sense of self...

Growing up isn't easy.

Time used to last forever...

Happily ever after's seemed possible,

Imaginations ran wild...

Then weeks turned to months,

Months turned into years,

Fiscally arranging themselves to control your movement.

"I can't do this yet, there isn't enough time", you tell yourself.

You're scheduled up unto the very last second.

"I'm doing this for you", you say to your future self....

Not realizing the time you've kept yourself from living is deterring the self you have yet to become.

Growing up...isn't easy.

In time it will come, is what I'm trying to tell you.

Starving your life of what it craves the most creates more harm than good.

Live now, don't rush to grow up...because...

It isn't easy.

A Friend

Dining at a table across from the person who has taught me so much from a far distance.

Looking at him, I realized I owed him an apology.

I needed to confess that my anger toward the title he was supposed to hold.

It tainted my perception of the man that is in front of me.

I held his mistakes like hot coals to be used to burn his name.

But for the first time I saw him for the man he was, a hurt, confused, and regretful man.

Once full of promise and life...

Wanting and needing to return to what once was.

I felt a sense of guilt but a sigh of relief.

Once my eyes were opened and my heart listened, I finally realized he needed a friend.

So use to closing off, I wonder if he'd accept me as such.

Not to reconcile our previous title, but start anew.

Clean slate. Wiping away all mistakes made and we begin again.

I wonder if a father would accept his daughter as a friend.

Momma

I wish I knew how to construct this poem to describe my
momma.
Words can't define how much she means to me. Like that's my
momma.
If you know us, you know that we have been all we have since
I was born.
The older I get and the more I pay attention, I see her more
now as a human than the superwoman that she has been to me
for the last 24 years.
Daily she reminds me I am her baby—I rebel her attempts to
"baby me" but I would be so mad if she treated me any
differently.
I wish I could show you how much I wanted to be like her. I
never tell her because I am scared to admit it. Why? I don't
know. I just am.
It irritates the crap out of me that she can do things I try so
hard to do with ease.
It bothers me more when she gives to others without a second
thought.
Why haven't I inherited that trait?

This petite woman holds so much fire and spunk, it's crazy. She lights up any room she walks in. She embraces my friends like they are her very own.

I love that about her.

And honestly, her honesty could break me down but lift me up all in one blow. I can't do anything but respect it.

I love this woman with all my heart.

When they call me "little Diane", I smile, because that's my momma...

Invasion

It's amazing how over a week's time you've invaded my
thoughts
Made a place in a space I never knew existed.
I cherish the time we've spent talking, laughing, and observing
each other's personalities.
I wish to continue this further.
I respect your time and hope you respect mine as well.
Equally we view each other with compassion hoping to gain
satisfaction from the space we share.
Come to me.
Listen to my heart beat steadily as you near.
It's insane, within this short amount of time I think I may have
fallen for you.
I hope you feel the same way too.

Love Me Back To Life

There were days when I just didn't think this relationship thing
was for me.
I dated, hung out with some but none of them could keep my
attention.
None of them could make me laugh at myself
Or look pass their flaws long enough to even consider them
wholly.
Then I met you.
You had this confidence that radiated through your walk,
The way you spoke and even your laugh.
I wouldn't say love at first sight, more like first encounter.
When you held me in your arms for the very first time
I felt safe secure and a sense of belonging.
You squeezed me so gently,
Kissed me so softly
The feeling resonated through my body like a bell being rung.
I wanted more, I wanted it all.
You looked me in my eyes told me I was beautiful.
My strong demeanor didn't frighten you, my emotions tend to
take control of my words but you never ran.

I'm glad God blessed me with you.

Courage & Love

I had a dream once about the two things this world can't live
without,
Courage and love.
In my dream, courage was a hard worker, risk taker, and
foundation of their union.
Love, on the other hand was what brought it all together,
Like the glue.
So sacred and pure,
Courage did everything its power to protect love.
Courage surrounded love to guard it from lies and deception.
They were the perfect team...
Their organic bond infiltrated everything in its reach.
Like a seedling sprouting roots, they grounded themselves in a
dark place with anticipation to one day blossom into the
beckon of hope this world cries for.

Courage and love. That was my dream.

Admiration

Why are you touching my spirit with your words?

I'm reading your phrases--each line exposes the girl I thought I

grew out of.

Scenarios of the past are being thrown back in my face.

Suppressed feelings have to be felt again.

Gosh man...

I am writing this in admiration.

I admire how attentive you are in aligning metaphors.

Your rhymes are like the cadences of my favorite beat—making

me question my decisions.

It's like my favorite lines questioning my religion,

Like my favorite verses renewing my faith.

Thank you sir.

Thank you for using your words to touch a part of me I

thought I rid myself of.

Because of you, this girl can create again,

Because of you, I believe in HIM.

Exposed

Many times I prayed to You covered.
Masking all my issues and challenges, thinking I can handle it all
alone.
My knees don't break to call Your name as they should...
but they easily get weak when a man who doesn't value me
shows the slightest attention.
It's easy for me to bare my all to the world, who critique my
body, my life, my ideas, and degrades my beauty, but I could
never show myself to You.
You're holy, this is a sacred space, I want to respect that... I
can't come to You with the perverted thoughts my mind
creates. I can't possibly fill Your space with my negativity and
dirt. It wouldn't be right to.

Then You shined Your light on me--revealing every secret,
every lie.
Like a federal agent busting through my door, You entered my
soul!
Uncovering all of my impure thoughts and You replaced them
with Yours. You set my dreams on fire to protect them from
the world's destruction. You arrested my heart. My heart that

turned cold with every passing year. You embraced me, every inconceivable part of me. You loved me like I've never been loved…

The mission to hide from You has been compromised.

I have been exposed.

Time

Time.

Moments we've shared in a space, seconds we've wasted.

Time.

A concept taken for granted, often rushed with the theory it

will bring us more value.

Time.

A simple word that holds complexity.

Time.

We don't have time,

I wish there were more TIME.

Stop what you're doing just live in this second, minute, and

hour.

This is your time.

On Purpose

For once I can admit that I did it all on purpose.

I looked you in your eyes and deceived you.

Manipulated you like pieces to a chess board.

You thought it was by fate that the ones you let in played you

consecutively?

No, sweetie, it was all me. I made you question your ability.

I compared you to that actress and those models.

I made you feel worthless...

Baby girl trust it wasn't in vain.

I did it with a master plan in mind. The journey I led you on

bruised you but made you stronger.

I led you to the ultimate protector; He gave you wisdom and

peace in a chaotic world.

Purposely, I did this for you. I wanted you to walk a path

unlike any other,

Run a race competing against none...but you.

On purpose I wanted you to see you for who He has created

you to be.

A true testament of His power and glory.

An example to that young girl, that woman, who sees you daily.

Have you looked at you lately?

I did this on purpose.

She

She lines her eyes that cried tears of uncertainty
Paints her lips with hope,
Remembering that the power of life lies on her tongue
Like ammo ready to be fired off unto God's ears.
She steps back...
Reviews her reflection.
Admiring every flawless imperfection,
Imagining her future like a vision...
"I am blessed" she tells herself.
But for the first time she sees what God sees
True beauty, love, and hope.
She forgives herself and walks into her destiny.